Printed in Great Britain
by Amazon

82650517R00079